MARRAKESH CONFIDENTIAL

HIDDEN GEMS LOVED BY LOCALS

JONGLEZ PUBLISHING

Travel guides

'THERE ARE FEW CITIES IN THE WORLD THAT BEWITCH YOU AS POWERFULLY AND WITH THE SAME MAGIC AS MARRAKESH. THERE ARE FEW CITIES AND FEW COUNTRIES THAT GIVE SO MUCH.'

PIERRE BERGÉ

LE
PROPHÈTE

How can you capture the soul of Marrakesh?

For the two of us – both in love with Morocco and both journeying between Marrakesh and our respective countries of exile – this is at once one of the most intriguing and difficult questions. We've scoured the nooks and crannies of this captivating city in order to distil the most striking and unexpected experiences. Out of the more than 1,000 places and experiences we tested, we selected just 30.

Yves St Laurent's private library, the best orange juice in the legendary Jamaa el-Fna square, the most beautiful riads and the best restaurants far from the tourist crowds, the search for the perfect carpet, a night in a tent in the desert, a secret museum where everything is for sale ...

Far from the well-trodden paths of Marrakesh, we invite you to immerse yourself in the more intimate side of this extraordinary city, discover its best-kept secrets and enjoy the most offbeat, intense experiences ... In the words of the Spanish writer and poet Juan Goytisolo, 'If you let yourself fall under the spell of Marrakesh, everywhere else in the world will seem boring.'

Rihlat saeida

Bon voyage !

WHAT YOU WON'T FIND IN THIS GUIDE

- the best place to ride a camel
- all-inclusive hotels
- how to pour mint tea
- tips for haggling
- a detailed map of the Medina

WHAT YOU WILL FIND IN THIS GUIDE

- the phone number of the best second-hand dealer in Marrakesh
- a playlist of the best Moroccan sounds
- local artists' best-loved greasy spoons
- the city's most beautiful hidden corners and most charming riads
- the locals' favourite spots in the Medina
- the art of making perfume

SYMBOLS OF
MARRAKESH

100–300
Moroccan
dirhams

300–500
Moroccan
dirhams

500–2,000
Moroccan
dirhams

You need a car
to get here

Reservation
recommended

Cash
only

Ask a local!

Opening times often vary,
so we recommend checking them directly
on the website of the place you plan to visit.

01. The most beautiful riads in La Medina
02. An unlikely flea market
03. Concoct the perfume of your dreams
04. The 'Picasso' of the Medina
05. The cultural oasis
06. In search of the perfect carpet
07. Some of our favourite restaurants in La Medina
08. A wonderful antique shop that feels like a museum
09. A hub for artistic encounters in a 19th-century riad
10. One thousand and one rooftops
11. Play it like Prince
12. Black soap, scrubbing and reconnecting with yourself
13. The best restaurants in Guéliz
14. Art walk in Marrakesh
15. The slow-fashion prodigy
16. Spices on the rocks
17. Wild about greasy spoons
18. Dive into the Kesh's artsy and electro side
19. Feminist couscous activists
20. An enigmatic library open by appointment only
21. The most beautiful hotels in La Palmeraie
22. A unique artistic experience
23. Made in Marrakesh
24. An oasis of calm 15 minutes from the centre
25. A garden as a surrealist work of art
26. Rooms you'll remember for the rest of your life

OUED
TENSIF
BAB
EL
KHEMIS
PALMERAIE
MEDINA
SOUK
KOUTOUBIA
ATLAS
TAXI

PHOTOS © L'HÔTEL MARRAKECH

#01

THE MOST BEAUTIFUL RIADS
IN LA MEDINA

> **Hotel Marrakech: a riad like no other**

In the heart of the Medina, just a few steps from the Koutoubia, Hotel Marrakech ranks among the finest riads in the city. Jasper Conran's vision has produced six beautiful suites wrapped around a garden and a swimming pool – something of a rarity in the Medina. Head up to the rooftop terrace for sweeping views of the Atlas Mountains over breakfast or late afternoon tea.

L'HÔTEL MARRAKECH
41 DERB SIDI LAHCEN OU ALI
BAB DOUKKALA

+212 5 24 38 78 80 | Instagram: @lhotelmarrakech | l-hotelmarrakech.com contact@l-hotelmarrakech.com

© IGOR DEMBA

> **Riad El Fenn: an oasis in the Medina**

Divided into several riads, El Fenn is considered one of the city's most beautiful hotels, its every detail a perfect combination of luxury and authenticity. The decor, colours, fabrics and furnishings are constantly revamped to provide a new experience each time you visit. Make sure to check out the sumptuous rooftop, a perfect perch from which to gaze out over the Medina.

EL FENN
DERB MOULAY ABDELLAH BEN HEZZIAN,
BAB EL KSOUR

Dh Dh Dh

+212 5 24 44 12 20	Instagram: @elfennmarrakech	contact@el-fenn.com el-fenn.com

© KASIA GATKOWSKA

PHOTOS © YVES DURONSOY

> **Riad de Tarabel: the villa suspended in time**

Time seems to have stood still at Riad de Tarabel, with its tree-lined patios, intimate atmosphere and birds of paradise. A former colonial residence, this house for aesthetes evokes refinement and calm in a decor that subtly blends vestiges of Arab-Andalusian architecture with a Second Empire style. A delicious sense of idleness, as in the golden age of the Red City. And superb cooking, exclusively for guests.

TARABEL MARRAKECH
DAR EL BACHA
8 DERB SRAGHNA

SPA
see page 77

Dh Dh

+212 5 24 39 17 06

contact@tarabelmarrakech.com
tarabelmarrakech.com
Instagram: @tarabelmarrakech

RIAD TARABEL

© YVES DURONSOY

> Riad Malika: the riad with flair

In the heart of one of the most beautiful districts of the Medina, home to antique dealers and the Dar el Bacha Palace, lies Riad Malika. In an oasis of pink bougainvillea and orange trees, this unusual bourgeois home holds many surprises, starting with its artwork and furniture, which reveal a pronounced penchant for the great designers of the 20th century.

RIAD MALIKA
29 ARSET AOUZAL
DAR EL BACHA

Dh Dh

+212 5 24 38 54 51

contact@riadmalika.com
riadmalika.com

> **Riad Farnatchi: 'the original'**

Since 2004, Riad Farnatchi has grown from a small B&B into a luxurious five-star hotel on a human scale. It features a dozen rooms (each more sumptuous than the next), a superlative spa and one of the city's most sought-after restaurants. Here, attention to detail is a philosophy and ensuring guests' well-being a way of life.

LE FARNATCHI
DERB EL FARNATCHI
RUE SOUK EL FASSIS
QUA'AT BEN AHID

Dh Dh Dh

+212 5 24 38 49 10	Instagram: @le_farnatchi	info@lefarnatchi.com lefarnatchi.com

> **Le Jardin Djahane: the hidden secret of the Medina**

This luxurious traditional 18th-century riad is named after Djahane, the revered lover of Persian poet Omar Khayyam. Five suites and four heavenly gardens invite you to enjoy a divine respite in the Bab Aylen district in the heart of the old Medina. A true love nest, where you can relax surrounded by the palm trees, turtles and chameleons that have made this place their own.

LE JARDIN DJAHANE
32 DERB CAID RASSOU

Dh Dh

+212 6 48 50 81 69	Instagram: @lejardindjahane	lejardindjahane@gmail.com lejardindjahane.com

PHOTOS © JARDIN DJAHANE

#02

AN UNLIKELY **FLEA MARKET**

Just outside the Medina, in a neighbourhood whose charm is not immediately apparent, El Khamis souk is something of a hidden gem. Tucked away among everyday items of little interest to most visitors are some of the city's most fascinating antique shops. In fact, dealers from around the world come here to stock up on ancient doors, 1950s film equipment, old lamps and much more.

While prices are lower than elsewhere in Marrakesh, haggling is, of course, an absolute must.

BAB EL KHEMIS

SAT–THU: 10am / 7pm

SOUK ALKHAMIS

#03

CONCOCT **THE PERFUME OF YOUR DREAMS**

In a 19th-century riad in the heart of the Medina, perfumer Abderrazzak Benchaâbane has created a space dedicated to the scents of Morocco: the Musée du Parfum (Perfume Museum).

From distillation to bottling, you'll learn everything there is to know about this delicate art as you wander through the rooms of the museum. If you're feeling daring, you can even try your hand at composing your own scent in one of the creative workshops, or have your ideal fragrance concocted at the perfume bar. The museum also organises 'olfactory awakening' workshops for children so that grown-ups can immerse themselves in their own sensory experience uninterrupted.

MUSÉE DU PARFUM
2 DERB CHÉRIF, DIOUR SABOUN

+212 5 24 38 74 84

museeduparfummarrakech@gmail.com
benchaabane.com

© MUSÉE DU PARFUM MARRAKECH

#04

THE 'PICASSO' OF THE MEDINA

In the cramped but very busy studio of this elderly Marrakesh painter, Monsieur Mourtaji, you'll find portraits of every king who has ruled Morocco, but also of icons such as our old friend, the Mona Lisa ... Slightly surreal, naive and touching, Mourtaji's works are known throughout the Medina.

Come and visit this little shop devoted to painting ... on canvas, on teapots and on anything that a paintbrush can embellish.

STUDIO M. MOURTAJI
SOUIKA DU RIAD LAAROUSS

18
TRICK 54

#05

THE CULTURAL OASIS

Founded in September 2013 by the brilliant Laila Hida, Le 18 is an independent platform for creation, dissemination, and cultural and artistic exchange. Unique in Marrakesh and hidden in the Medina, this collective seeks to support emerging artists by offering them residencies, as well as by disseminating and exhibiting their work to the public. The perfect place to discover new talent from Marrakesh.

LE 18
18 DERB EL FERRANE, RIAD LAAROUSS

Dh Dh

Instagram: @le18marrakech | le18marrakech@gmail.com

- LAILA HIDA -

CREATOR OF LE 18

Tell us more about your intentions when launching Le 18 – how it came to life and how it continues to thrive today.

It was intuitive, born from a desire to do and to share. The aim was to provide a creative space for other artists, researchers, curators and the general public. Le 18 evolved over time: it's similar to Moroccan houses, which usually start with two rooms, and then more rooms and living spaces are added as the family grows. In my opinion, the architecture of a cultural project should resemble this growing family whose space interacts with the need to respond to a given context.

Besides Le 18, which cultural spaces or institutions are doing a good job supporting young artists today?

Dar Bellarj, in the Medina of Marrakesh, works with a community of local women and, over time, has become an essential mediator between the young women and their families. Then there's On Marche, the yearly festival of contemporary African dance, which will host the Biennale de la Danse en Afrique (Africa Dance Biennale) in 2021. Jardin Rouge is opening its residencies to host more young local emerging artists. I must also mention L'Atelier de l'Observatoire in Casablanca; Think Tangier (based in Tangier) for their art and research residencies as well as their workshops; and the Cinémathèque de Tanger. I love the new Qisas project, which focuses on storytelling, photography and video. These past ten years have seen a significant expansion of the cultural scene through different projects, new residencies, artists' initiatives and institutions that have emerged all over the country. The structures are still fragile but they are managing to find their own model and ecosystems.

Tell us about your favourite meal in Marrakesh!

To eat quickly and very well on a small budget, the chicken *tanjia* and *loubia* at Snack Abderrahim on Boulevard Moulay Rachid are my favourites. With a group of other people, I've also recently undertaken to compile the ultimate guide to *loubia* in Marrakesh! For a treat (also in Guéliz), try +61 for the subtlety of a mixed Australian-Mediterranean cuisine, sometimes with Asian influences – simple but exquisite. In the Medina, the most beautiful spot for lunch is Le Jardin. I simply love the place, with its greenery and very relaxed atmosphere; I can stay there for hours.

Name your three absolute favourite spots in Marrakesh.

First, Café Imlil on Rue de la Liberté for my morning coffee and orange juice. Second, Maison ARTC, the studio and showroom of Artsi Ifrach, a talented and fantastically creative artist. He makes everything from clothes to photography, artworks and books. His place is a great source of inspiration to me. And, third, the booksellers of Bab Doukkala, where you can discover some real gems: books, old magazines, very old local journals and zines. My friend, the artist Noureddine Ezzaraf, found a whole collection of *Lamalif* (a political and cultural magazine published between 1966 and 1988) there: they are exhibited in my current show at Dar Belarj.

#06

IN SEARCH OF **THE PERFECT CARPET**

Talking about Moroccan artisanship without mentioning carpets is inconceivable. In Marrakesh, you'll find hundreds of shops selling more or less authentic carpets. We recommend a trip to the showrooms of Soufiane and Ismaïl Zarib, two brothers who have rugs in their blood, as it were. Foregoing shop windows and displays, their business runs by word of mouth. Inside, you'll find hundreds of carpets from the Beni Ourain, Taznakht and Boujad regions displayed in modern showrooms that will make you want to redo your interior. You're bound to find the rug of your dreams here.

SOFIANE ZARIB - SHOWROOM
16 RUE SIDI SLI BEN HAMDOUCH
DAR EL BACHA

SOFIANE ZARIB - WAREHOUSE
SIDI GHANEM

+212 6 15 28 56 90

Instagram: @soufiane.zarib

soufiane-zarib.com

ICON

- **Beni Ourain:** knotted wool carpet. Usually white and black, the patterns on these rugs are rather simple and presented graphically.

- **Azilal:** knotted wool carpet. Visually busier, these rugs can be very colourful or black and white.

- **Boujad:** highly original decorative item that should be considered a work of art. Some models take months to complete.

- **Boucherouite:** patchwork rug made of recycled materials such as fabric and scraps of clothing.

- **Beni Mguild:** made in the Middle Atlas Mountains, these carpets were originally designed for winter use and were valued for their excellent insulating properties.

- **Kilim:** rug from the Near East and Central Asia made of cotton and goat wool and woven using a technique dating back over 10,000 years.

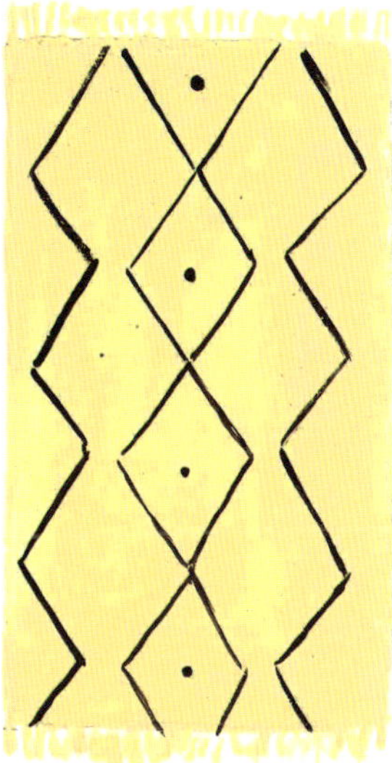

Beni Ourain

Azilal

Boujad

Boucherouite

Beni Mguild

Kilim

- AMINE BENDRIOUICH -

COUTURIER

Who are your favourite designers in Marrakesh?

Daniel Oiknine, from Métiers d'Hier: a passionate ironworker who practically lives in his workshop – he's always busy creating something. He was one of the late Pierre Bergé's favourite skilled artisans and developed several designs for him. His creations range from steampunk sculptures to industrial furniture.

Arzen is an impressive artisanal factory, founded and directed by Rachid, who has taken traditional production to new heights. When you see their brass products, you could swear they're laser cut … but every operation is actually done by hand, in a sophisticated yet simple way that's very close to poetry.

The bag designer Zakaria Bendriouich is one of Marrakesh's most innovative artisans, skilfully melding craft, design and art. He lost a kidney in an accident, meaning that he has to drink five litres of water a day ... This led to the creation of the Bido bag, literally a jerrycan bag made out of leather and upcycled plastic jerrycan parts. A whole collection followed, using the same methods and philosophy – the bags are worn by the likes of Naomi Campbell, to name just a few.

What do you reckon is the link between artisans and art?

My personal opinion might be controversial for many people, but I firmly believe that skilled craftsmanship used to be integrated with art, which in Morocco meant every aspect of life, from the utilitarian to the ornamental, from clothes to architecture, and so on. The separation between art and handicrafts occurred as a direct result of colonialism. Artisans started churning out only the designs that Westerners wanted and what they thought was beautiful. The painter Jacques Majorelle was given the task of setting up the first Moroccan artisanat office, which created this false separation. Today, more and more contemporary artists are moving closer to crafts, and more artisans are approaching their work from an artistic perspective. This will allow handicrafts to regain their original nature and status ... which is living art.

Twelve hours in Marrakesh with someone you're trying to impress?

09:30 – breakfast on the roof terrace of Shtatto, with its breathtaking views over the Medina and the entire mountain chain; then shopping in Shtatto's boutiques.

11:00 – visit to my shop, Welcome to the Kingdom.

11:30 – Moulay Youssef Lamdaghri's Bazar Coffre Mystérieux, then lunch here, prepared by Maalem Bana (this needs to be ordered one day in advance). Try Razzete Bana, his personal take on Moroccan mhancha and pastilla.

13:30 – Bazar du Sud, owned by the family who started the carpet business in Marrakesh in the 1930s as an act of resistance against the French occupation. They have some of the most unique rugs in all Morocco.

14:30 – Dar Bellarj Foundation, for whatever they're showing, from music to theatre, art and embroidery – it's generally worth the expense.

15:00 – Bert Flint Museum, one of the most splendid collections of Moroccan art.

15:45 – head out to the Medina through Riad Larousse Soui to stop at the tiny shop/atelier of Monsieur Mourtaji, one of my favourite painters in the Medina.

16:15 – Musée Farid Belkahia (Belkahia is one of the most important artists on the contemporary Moroccan scene).

17:45 – head to Kabana, the best thing that's happened to the Medina recently.
You can have a cocktail and tapas while listening to good music, with a view of the famous Koutoubia mosque and the surrounding gardens, enjoyed by lots of local people.

19:00 – dinner at Dar Simons, a fine-dining experience from a talented young Belgian chef with a subtle Moroccan influence.
Delicate and fun, with a story behind every dish.

21:00 – last stop at the legendary palace of La Mamounia. Should you head for the piano retro bar or the main bar by the lobby? It's a difficult choice!
But the palace was built for the prince Moulay Mamoun to enjoy nature, music and dance with his loved ones, and somehow you still get this atmosphere today, whatever you decide to do.

AMINE
BENDRIOUIC

#07

SOME OF OUR FAVOURITE **RESTAURANTS IN THE MEDINA**

For anyone who, after a few days, can't face another bite of couscous, this selection of spots is for you. On the menu: Australian, Lebanese, and vegetarian flavours, plus three places for a delicious, no-compromise break.

> **Restaurant Le Jardin**

In the heart of an old building dating from the 16th century, far from the hustle and bustle of the Medina, Le Jardin restaurant is set in the middle of a lush garden overlooked by tastefully furnished terraces and little lounges. On the menu: a modern fusion of Moroccan and European flavours.

Kamal Laftimi's second venture (after Café des Épices), Le Jardin also serves delicious cocktails at the end of the day, so you can take full advantage of the coolness of this small urban oasis.

RESTAURANT LE JARDIN
32 SOUK EL JELD SIDI ABDELAZIZ

+212 5 24 37 82 95	Instagram: @lejardinmarrakech	lejardinmarrakech.com

© LA FAMILLE

> Mandala

Le Mandala is a family affair and a love story between Moroccan and Scandinavian cuisine. An improbable culinary union that brings the best of both cultures, from 100% Arabica coffees to divinely smoked fish.

MANDALA SOCIETY 159 RUE RIAD ZITOUN EL JDID	MANDALA SOCIETY 20 BIS RUE KOUTOUBIA

+212 6 42 95 70 62	Instagram: @mandala_society	mandalasociety.co

> La Famille

What a delight to have lunch in the shade of the bougainvillea in La Famille's garden! Vegetarian, organic and ultra-fresh, the menu at this small, highly Instagrammable spot changes daily according to what's available at the market. And the temptations don't end there: there's also a boutique corner with a lovely selection of objects and jewellery by Stephanie Jewels.

LA FAMILLE
42 RUE RIAD ZITOUN EL JDID,
(NEXT TO THE BAHIA PALACE)

Reservations required on +212 5 24 38 52 95	Instagram: @la_famille_marrakech	lafamillemarrakech.com

LA FAMILLE © LA FAMILLE

> Villa Aaron

In a stunning 1930s house decorated with great subtlety by Michèle Rose, Villa Aaron recreates the atmosphere of a grand manor house with period crockery and vintage furniture, original tiles and ceramics, and painted ceilings and frescoes. The five magnificent drawing rooms are arranged around a blue and green patio whose walls are hand-painted with stylised palm trees and majestic peacocks. Fusion cuisine blending Mediterranean and Moroccan influences.

VILLA AARON
7 RUE IBN ROCHD

+212 6 69 09 08 28 | Instagram: @villa_aaron_marrakech | villa-aaron.com contact@villa-aaron.com

PHOTOS @ VILLA AARON

> **Dar Yacout**

Dar Yacout, one of the cult restaurants in the Medina, is not to be missed. Both its decor and its menu offer an excellent introduction to Moroccan culture. Renowned for its traditional dishes, this dinner-only institution has made a name for itself with a few local specialities: an almond chicken to die for and wonderful cinnamon oranges. Before you sit down to dinner, head up to the terrace to admire a view of the Koutoubia mosque against the setting sun.

DAR YACOUT
79 DERB SIDI AHMED SOUSSI,
BAB DOUKKALA

+212 5 24 38 29 29 | Instagram: @daryacoutmarrakech | reservation@daryacout.com daryacout.com

© DAR YACOUT

- AMINE KABBAJ -

ARCHITECT

You talk a lot about the context in which Marrakesh exists and without which it's impossible to fully grasp the city's historical importance. Which historical places define it?

The problem for me is that Marrakesh can't be defined by its centre alone. Marrakesh is also what's around this core. This is important because if you consider only the Medina, you disconnect yourself from its history. Marrakesh only makes sense within its context – and that context is the Atlas Mountains; Marrakesh was born from the Atlas Mountains. The first capital (before Marrakesh) was Aghmat, located 35 km to the south. Starting from there, the following sites are must-sees: the Yagour plateau and its rock carvings (a journey back in time to 5000 BC); the Great

Mosque of Tinmel (the foundation of the largest Moroccan empire under the Almohads); Aghmat (the birth of the Almoravids and their conquest of Spain); the Oued Tensift bridge (an often ignored work of art built by the Almoravids over 900 years ago); the Agdal and Menara gardens, with their water reservoirs for the olive groves; the Walls of Marrakesh; the Jbel Guéliz; the dry Oued Issil river, which divides Marrakesh from east to west; the Almoravid Qubba; the Koutoubia mosque; Dar el Bacha Palace, the residence of notables; Bahia Palace; Dar Si Said; El Badi Palace (a royal residence that rivals Versailles); the fountains where animals and humans drank; the Mellah (Jewish quarter); and the Saadian Tombs, a protected necropolis.

Which novels do you think best sum up the history of Morocco and Marrakesh?

Jacques Attali's *La confrérie des éveillés* (Brotherhood of the Awakened) and Gilbert Sinoué's *Averroès ou le secrétaire du diable* (Averroès or The Devil's Secretary). Ibn Tufail is also a must-read – he was the mentor of Ibn Rushd (or Averroes), who wrote in the late 12th century and inspired the character of Robinson Crusoe. I also strongly recommend the work of Nabil Mouline, an eminent young Moroccan historian, and of Ahmed Toufiq, Minister for Islamic Affairs, who is an excellent novelist and has written extensively on the history of Morocco.

AMINE KABBAJ'S GUIDE TO THE MEDINA

- **Belhaj**: for jewellery and traditional silver objects; next to Bab Ftouh and the Foundouk Ouarzazi Souk.

- **Chez Jilali**: a fantastic flea market, right next to the dyers. Belhaj and Jilali are two of the most traditional, authentic people.

- **Marché Subsaharien**: for beautiful sub-Saharan African fabrics, indigo and Ivorian and Senegalese textiles.

- **Abdelsakt Ouzid**: another quality flea market, next to the Mouassine mosque.

- **L'Atrach**: a recent silverware business. Items also sold by La Mamounia.

- **Soumia Kabbaj**: for traditional clothing.

- **Fatim Zahra bel Attar**: for dates, raisins, peanuts, etc.

- **Mishi**: a fun Japanese-Moroccan shop for unique clothing and objects. Moroccan handicrafts with a Japanese twist.

- **Hamid**: for authentic babouche slippers!

- **Khalid Art Gallery**: the Medina's luxury second-hand dealer, with five or six shops between the Medina and the Yves Saint Laurent Museum.

- **Pikala**: a very well-known and respected association in the Medina, founded by a Dutch woman. They offer training to young people in Marrakesh as professional bicycle tour guides; the bikes are just an excuse for discovering the city, a way to see it from a different perspective.

#08

A WONDERFUL ANTIQUE SHOP THAT FEELS LIKE A MUSEUM

A few steps from El Fenn, on this narrow street leading to the heart of the Medina, just before you reach the red café on your right, enter this palace from another era. Everything you see here is for sale.

In this labyrinth of antiques, you'll find centuries-old backgammon sets, improbable solid-wood thrones and Judaized Berber liturgical objects dating from before the Arab conquests. A veritable Ali Baba's cave, where time seems to stand still.

TRÉSOR DES MILLE ET UNE NUITS
22 RUE SIDI EL YAMANI

+212 6 61 38 34 67

#09

A HUB FOR ARTISTIC ENCOUNTERS
IN A 19TH-CENTURY RIAD

Just off Jemaa el Fnaa square, this late 19th-century riad is striking both for its sheer size (it spans over 1,000 m^2!) and its beautifully preserved architecture. Once home to Sultan Hassan I's treasurer, it now welcomes local children and teenagers for cultural and artistic programmes.

The project is the work of filmmaker Nabil Ayouch and artist Mahi Binebine, who established the Ali Zaoua Foundation in 2014 in an attempt to counter extremism through culture.

LES ÉTOILES DE JEMAÂ EL FNA
FONDATION ALI ZAOUA
36 DERB FHEL ZEFRITI

+212 5 24 38 02 21	Programme on Instagram: @lesetoiles_jemaaelfna	fondationalizaoua.org

Opened in late 2021, the Jemaa el Fnaa centre is the fifth of its kind, following those in Casablanca, Fès, Agadir and Tangier. Each year it welcomes more than 900 young people, mostly from Marrakesh's Medina. Designed as a place for learning, discovery, sharing and creative expression, it aims to build a real sense of community. Children can try their hand at some

© WASSIM-B

20 artistic pursuits including theatre, visual arts, chess, calligraphy, contemporary dance, piano, violin, graffiti and even DJing. Les Étoiles de Jemaa el-Fna doubles as a performance venue. An open stage at the heart of the riad welcomes artists from every discipline and background for shows, concerts and cultural exchanges, all free and open to the public through partnerships with international institutions.

#10

ONE THOUSAND AND ONE ROOFTOPS

After wandering at length through the narrow streets of the Medina, it's a good idea to retire to higher ground at the end of the day to enjoy the sunset. Moroccan architecture is conducive to the creation of fantastic outdoor spaces, and there are countless rooftops in Marrakesh. Here is our selection of high-perched places:

> **Le Kabana**

Just opposite the old Koutoubia mosque, this most recent addition to the rooftop landscape has quickly established itself as the cool and cosmopolitan landmark in the Medina. You can dine here (Mediterranean cuisine and a sushi bar) or just drop in to enjoy a cocktail to the sounds of a DJ set.

LE KABANA
KISSARIAT BEN KHALED R'MILA
1 RUE FATIMA ZAHRA

+212 6 64 46 44 50	Instagram: @kabana.marrakech	kabana-marrakech.com

> **L'Mida**

Tucked away just a stone's throw from the Place des Épices, Omar and Simo's restaurant combines Marrakesh tradition with a taste for simple things. This Moroccan restaurant is as friendly as it is trendy and you'll relish lounging on the large green benches while waiting for your lunch.

L'MIDA
78 BIS DERB NKHEL

Dh Dh

Reservations on +212 5 24 44 36 62	Instagram: @lmidamarrakech	lmidamarrakech.com

PHOTOS © MÖ-MÖ

> MÖ-MÖ

With its two terraces overlooking Jemaa el Fnaa square, MÖ-MÖ is a lovely spot from which to watch the activity below. Yann Dobry created the deliberately maximalist interior. Quality Mediterranean cuisine.

MÖ-MÖ
1 RIAD ZITOUN LAKDIM

Dh

+212 6 66 42 06 40

#09

PLAY IT
LIKE PRINCE

Aya's, a small made-to-measure clothing boutique, has been on a quiet street in the Medina since 2001. Its founder, Nawal el Hariti, has built an international reputation – Prince himself was one of her customers ...

If you have something specific in mind, you've come to the right place. After a brainstorming session, head to the souk to buy fabric and ornaments, then back to the studio for fittings and lunch with the designer. Then wait a few days and, voilà, your divine outfit awaits you!

SHOP AYA'S MARRAKESH

+212 6 61 46 29 16 | Instagram: @ayasmarrakech | ayasmarrakech.com

#12

BLACK SOAP, SCRUBBING **AND RECONNECTING WITH YOURSELF**

An age-old institution and a Middle Eastern beauty ritual, going to the hammam is a not-to-be-missed experience in Marrakesh. To shed your old skin, treat yourself to an hour or more of soaping down, scrubbing and massage in this haven of relaxation. An excellent way to take a breather from your exploration of the bustling Moroccan city.

> **La Sultana Spa: the hammam of kings**

This spa, located in Marrakesh's smallest five-star hotel, La Sultana, could be straight out of a palace in *The Arabian Nights*. In this architectural gem, the washing rituals take place around an antique pool made of pink marble. A luxurious space designed to satisfy the most demanding of customers.

lasultanahotels.com

ARGAN

> **Les Bains de Marrakech: the most local hammam**

Recently renovated, this Marrakesh institution retains the purely traditional character of an authentic Middle Eastern hammam. Enjoy a salt crystal or sugar scrub, rhassoul ritual or scented bath.

lesbainsdemarrakech.com

> **Les Bains de Tarabel: lose track of time**

Nowhere have the traditional Maghreb beauty secrets been better kept than at Les Bains de Tarabel. Next to the hotel of the same name, this cosy hammam offers a wonderful moment of relaxation seemingly outside the stream of time. We recommend the foot bath with sea salts and bitter orange essence.

lesbainsdetarabel.com

> **Royal Mansour: the ultimate hammam experience**

Owned by the King of Morocco, the Royal Mansour is one of the most exclusive places in Marrakesh. Inside, you'll discover a spectacular hammam and custom-made treatments so you can try out the Red City's age-old rituals for yourself.

royalmansour.com/marrakech

LES BAINS DE TARABEL © YVES DURONSOY

LES BAINS DE MARRAKECH © M|Y BRAND DESIGN

#13

THE BEST RESTAURANTS
IN GUÉLIZ

> **Azar**

Hummus, falafel, kibbeh, tzatziki ... When you go to Azar, it's because you're hankering for an excellent Lebanese alternative. Warmed by the scent of shisha smoke, the atmosphere is hushed, until oriental dancers liven things up at 10 pm. Let yourself be buoyed up too.

AZAR
RUE DE YOUGOSLAVIE
(ON THE PART OF BOULEVARD HASSAN II)

Dh Dh

+212 5 24 43 09 20 | Instagram: @azarmarrakech | azarmarrakech.com

PHOTOS © FARMERS

> **Farmers**

In the Galerie El Beqal, Guéliz's Art Deco arcade, Farmers serves food sourced from the organic Sanctuary Slimane farm in a beautifully designed space with an open kitchen, decorated with green zellige tiles and brass touches. While you're there, explore the rest of the gallery, which also houses Restaurant +61 (see p. 86), the Booklore bookshop and the Blue Ribbon bistro.

FARMERS
96 RUE MOHAMED EL BEQAL

+212 5 24 42 30 22	Instagram: @farmersmarrakech	farmersmarrakech.com

> **Pétanque Social Club**

In the heart of Guéliz, the Pétanque Social Club (PSC) has brought a 1930s club back to life, transforming it into a sprawling, convivial garden designed for whiling away time between games of petanque, cocktails and excellent music. Very decent Mediterranean food and a young, festive atmosphere.

PÉTANQUE SOCIAL CLUB
70 BOULEVARD EL MANSOUR EDDAHBI

+212 6 66 45 53 80	Instagram: @psc_marrakech	pscmarrakech.com booking@pscmarrakech.com

BACARDI
APEROL
CAMPARI

> +61

Simple, generous and relaxed, chef Andrew Cibej's cuisine consists of the best of Australian gastronomy. No fuss, all flavour.

+61
96 RUE MOHAMED EL BEQAL

plus61.com

#14

ART WALK
IN MARRAKESH

As Marrakesh begins to make a name for itself in the international art market, galleries are proliferating in the city centre, especially in the trendy Guéliz district. Here's a little cultural jaunt through the area that we've put together for you.

> Comptoir des Mines Gallery

Nestled in a 1930s Art Deco building, the Comptoir des Mines is part of Marrakesh's historical and cultural heritage. Transformed into an art centre, it has become the point of reference for the new Moroccan art scene. Don't miss it – both the works and the building are worth a visit.

COMPTOIR DES MINES
62 CORNER OF RUE DE LA LIBERTÉ
AND RUE DE YOUGOSLAVIE, GUÉLIZ

+212 6 88 14 60 74 | Instagram: @cmgmarrakech | cmgmarrakech.com

PHOTOS © COMPTOIR DES MINES

> Tindouf Gallery

Established in 2007, Galerie Tindouf has built a reputation in the field of contemporary and fine arts. Its unique pieces by renowned artisans and artists are carefully selected by curator Boubker Temli, who can also tell you the story behind them.

TINDOUF GALLERY
22 BOULEVARD MOHAMMED VI
GUÉLIZ

+212 5 24 43 09 08 | galerietindouf.com

> Loft Art Gallery

The Guéliz neighbourhood is home to Loft Art Gallery, the Marrakesh branch of a gallery founded in Casablanca in 2009 by Myriem and Yasmine Berrada Sounni, focusing on modern and contemporary art from Morocco and across Africa. The gallery regularly showcases painting, photography and installation works, and champions artists such as Amina Agueznay and Amina Rezki (Agueznay has been selected to represent Morocco at the 2026 Venice Biennale).

LOFT ART GALLERY
60 BOULEVARD EL MANSOUR EDDAHBI
GUÉLIZ

+212 5 22 94 47 65	Instagram: @loftartgallery	loftartgallery.net

© AYOUB EL BARDII / MCC GALLERY

> MCC Gallery

Founded by Fatima-Zohra Bennani Bennis (who in 2018 established Dar El Bacha, considered Morocco's first gallery dedicated to photography), MCC Gallery is a contemporary art space covering some 600 m². It was designed as a platform for experimentation and dialogue between Moroccan and international artists. Regular exhibitions open to the public are held throughout the year.

MCC GALLERY
281, RUE PRINCIPALE, SIDI GHANEM

+212 8 08 59 59 99	Instagram: @mcc_galery	mcc-gallery.com

> Rigotang

An offshoot of the artistic residency programme at Riad Jardin Secret (also worth a visit), Rigotang Gallery was created by the same owners to provide a second exhibition space for works produced in Marrakesh by artists hosted at the riad.

RIGOTANG
278, RUE PRINCIPALE, SIDI GHANEM

By appointment only
+212 6 67 24 48 09

Instagram: @rigotang
rigotang.com
Riad Jardin Secret: riadjardinsecret.com

> Al Maqam

Located in Tahanaout, about 30 km from Marrakesh, this artists' residence, created by the painter Mohamed Mourabiti, is a unique and extremely versatile place. A meeting point for local creatives, Al Maqam is also a gallery, literary café and restaurant, lost in a sea of olive trees.

AL MAQAM
EL MGASSEM,
MARRAKECH TENSIFT AL HAOUZ,
42302 TAHANNAOUT

+212 5 24 48 40 02

Instagram: @almaqamartistresidence

#15

THE SLOW-FASHION
PRODIGY

Born in Jerusalem, the designer Artsi Ifrach settled in Morocco after wandering between Tel Aviv, Paris and Amsterdam. A professional classical dancer, this Marrakshi-at-heart came to fashion later in life. He is passionate about art, history and materials, and his brand ARTC reflects his multiculturalism: rich, colourful and eclectic. The slow pace of Marrakesh has rubbed off on his practice, turning him into a follower of 'slow fashion'. His creations are made of vintage fabrics found in markets around the world, and his inspirations are as far-ranging as his travel diaries. Make sure to visit his showroom in the Guéliz district: Artsi will be there to welcome you.

MAISON ARTC BY ARTSI IFRACH
4 BOULEVARD EL MANSOUR EDDAHBI
GUÉLIZ

Dh Dh

Make an appointment on
+212 6 65 03 55 10

Instagram: @maisonartc

info@maisonartc.com
maisonartc.com

أمل

MAISON ARTC

#16

SPICES **ON THE ROCKS**

The huge iron 'B' hides a small staircase leading to one of the trendiest places in Guéliz: Le Baromètre. With its decor reminiscent of an early 20th-century American speakeasy, Morocco's first mixology bar will intoxicate you with its retro atmosphere and incredible cocktails.

Leaning on the counter, you can watch the drink you've ordered being made, step by step, subtly enhanced with spices, aromatic herbs, floral waters and macerated fruits.

An exotic liquid garden of sorts that you can sip in a very New York atmosphere.

BAR LE BAROMÈTRE
RUE MOULAY ALI

+212 6 66 88 67 98

lebarometre.net
Instagram: @barometremarrakech

To register for mixology courses and for more info: inforesa@lebarometre.net

#17

WILD ABOUT **GREASY SPOONS**

You can't judge a country's culinary culture without trying its greasy spoons. They're legion in Marrakesh. These are our favourites (forget what they look like from the outside; you'll just have to trust us on this).

> Chez Bejgueni

Hands down, one of the best places for grilled lamb chops. Tourists are welcomed like locals here, with straightforward and friendly service.
21 rue Ibn Aïcha, Guéliz
Daily: 10am / 10pm

> Chez Ouazzani

Meat lovers shouldn't miss this small restaurant in Guéliz. The dishes are hearty and bursting with flavour, the prices decidedly affordable.
12 bis rue Ibn Aïcha, Guéliz
Daily: noon / 2am

> Al Bahriya

Marrakesh natives have been licking their fingers in delight at this little seafood eatery for almost 30 years. Choose what you want from the large stand and it will be sent over to the plancha before finally landing on your plate.
75 boulevard Moulay Rachid
Daily: 11:45am / 1am

PERADOS

#18

DIVE INTO THE KESH'S **ARTSY AND ELECTRO SIDE**

Drink, Art, Food & Music is the motto of l'Envers, Marrakesh's one and only electro bar. Since its opening in 2017, party-goers have made it their headquarters, flocking here to dance to the sounds of the city's best DJs. An artsy spot par excellence, l'Envers also attracts lovers of photography and street art, who come to admire the temporary exhibitions on the walls. Others just want to meet up with friends and chill in a great atmosphere. The crowd is cosmopolitan, the cocktails well shaken, the food comforting. Go all in.

L'ENVERS
29 RUE IBN AÏCHA, GUÉLIZ

Dh Dh

+212 6 62 55 24 78

Instagram: @lenversmarrakech

#19

FEMINIST
COUSCOUS ACTIVISTS

Fridays are for couscous! But not just anywhere. Head to one of the centres of the association Amal, dedicated to empowering women in disadvantaged situations. Thanks to reintegration programmes, women who are divorced, widowed, single or have dependent children can develop their skills, especially in the kitchen. Have lunch here or, better still, learn to cook your favourite Moroccan dish in the company of these incredible women. Reservations are recommended.

ASSOCIATION AMAL
RUE ALLAL BEN AHMED
AND RUE IBN SINA

+212 5 24 44 68 96	amalnonprofit.org Instagram: @amalnonprofit	Make reservations online for the workshops More information on +212 5 24 49 37 76

امل
amal

امل

Myrian.C

#20

AN ENIGMATIC LIBRARY
OPEN BY APPOINTMENT ONLY

Yves Saint Laurent has left a tremendous legacy in Marrakesh. In addition to the Majorelle Garden, the sumptuous Villa Oasis and an incredible art collection, the French couturier left behind an enigmatic research library housed inside the Yves Saint Laurent Museum. Packed with rare books, it's open (by appointment only) to anyone who can justify a serious interest in the archives. While many of the books are about Morocco, the library also holds special collections on the legendary designer and on fashion. In preparation for your visit, have a look at the online catalogue.

BIBLIOTHÈQUE DU MUSÉE YVES SAINT LAURENT
RUE YVES SAINT LAURENT

+212 5 24 29 86 86 | museeyslmarrakech.com/fr/bibliotheque

TIFINAGH
OR THE BEAUTY OF THE BERBER ALPHABET

Strange geometric symbols engraved in stone nearly 3,000 years ago are the oldest traces of what is now called the Tifinagh alphabet, whose origins remain as mysterious as its almost extraterrestrial aesthetic. After falling into disuse and then being reintroduced 30 years ago, this alphabet is still used to write Tamazight, the language spoken by Berber populations in North Africa.

The Tuareg, 'the blue men of the Sahara', are currently the only Berber-speaking people to actively use the Tifinagh script, though many Moroccans speak Tamazight. In fact, over a quarter of the kingdom's population uses one of the country's three main Berber dialects (Tarifit, Tamazight and Tachelhit). But across North Africa, where Berbers have lived for centuries and still live today, many other languages are spoken, including Nafusi, Siwi and Zenaga. Moroccan multiculturalism is a reflection of these ancient populations: tenacious and mixed.

#21

THE MOST BEAUTIFUL **HOTELS IN LA PALMERAIE**

Marrakesh has countless charming hotels. But don't worry, you won't need to spend hours online to find that rare gem: we've compiled a selection of the best addresses for you.

> **Ksar Char-Bagh: the old Andalusian Palace**

Ksar Char-Bagh is a small private palace set in the heart of Marrakesh's beautiful Palmeraie. From the large Moorish patio, you can admire the fountains and the citrus and olive groves that stretch as far as the eye can see in the hotel's vast park. After dark, immerse yourself in the books in the art library or head to the old smoking lounge, which encourages visitors to share their secrets. A place brimming with history, where every passing day is a journey in itself.

KSAR CHAR-BAGH
LA PALMERAIE
ROUTE DE FÈS

+212 5 24 32 92 44

resa@ksarcharbagh.fr
ksarcharbagh.fr

> Jnane Tamsna: the secret garden in Palmeraie ▲

The Jnane Tamsna riad combines elegant interior design by Meryanne Loum-Martin (as chic here as in her hotel) with the serenity of a garden under the care of her botanist husband, Gary Martin. A fusion of architecture and nature that makes this boutique hotel one of a kind – friendly yet mysterious, just like its creators.

JNANE TAMSNA
DOUAR ABIAD
LA PALMERAIE

+212 5 24 32 84 84	Instagram: @jnanetamsna	requests@jnanetamsna.com jnanetamsna.com

© JNANE TAMSNA

> **Casa Gyla: the romantic villa**

In the middle of the golden triangle of Marrakesh's Palmeraie lies the mysterious Casa Gyla, an Arab-Andalusian villa built by the architect Jacqueline Foissac and her lover, the Spanish painter Alejandro Reino. In the shade of cypress trees, the house nestles in a lush garden dotted with bougainvillea, century-old olive trees and rosebushes that spread their intoxicating perfume along the paths of the park.

CASA GYLA
VILLA HAROUCHI
ROUTE DES JARDINS DE LA PALMERAIE

+212 5 24 71 98 34

> **Jnane Rumi: a well-kept secret**

Just ten minutes from the bustle of the Medina, tucked away in the heart of a palm grove, Jnane Rumi is a closely guarded secret. Part artists' residence, part insider's retreat, this intimate twelve-room property designed by architect Charles Boccara blends Moroccan craftsmanship with contemporary design, complemented by an impressive art collection.

The rooms are beautiful: traditional architecture meets raw materials in a palette of beiges, ochres and off-whites, punctuated by vibrant touches of olive green, terracotta, mustard yellow and carmine red.

JNANE RUMI
RUE ASSAWSSAN 2
NAKHIL NORD PALMERAIE

+212 5 24 32 87 51	From €350 per night	jnanerumi.com info@jnanerumi.com Instagram: @jnanerumi

© DAVID DUMON / JNANE RUMI

Each room has its own personality.

The Majnun suite is particularly striking, with its Majorelle blue paying homage to Marrakesh's iconic garden. For the ultimate indulgence, book the Rabia annexe: a 53-square-metre private sanctuary with its own garden and pool, a four-poster bed and a copper bathtub, decorated throughout with works by Amina Benbouchta.

The gardens are filled with fig, olive and pistachio trees, and it's here that chef Moula Erraissi (formerly of +61, see p. 146) reinvents Moroccan cuisine with flair under the culinary direction of Karin Gaasterland. At lunch, enjoy seasonal small plates in the shade of the palms or on a secluded terrace. Come evening, tuck into contemporary takes on traditional tagines beneath the stars.

Time seems to slow down here, and you'll find yourself never wanting to leave. This is Marrakesh at its most serene – a place where you can rediscover the true luxury of doing nothing at all.

ALBERTO PINTO

#22

A UNIQUE
ARTISTIC EXPERIENCE

Created by visual artist Jean-François Fourtou, Villa Dar El Sadaka and its grounds have recently opened to visitors.

Twenty minutes from the Medina, in the heart of Marrakesh's Palmeraie, a visit to Dar El Sadaka is a unique artistic experience. You'll find a giant's house where all the furniture and objects are twice normal size, a house that's 'fallen from the sky' with its roof on the ground and everything upside down, and surreal animal sculptures throughout the gardens.

RAMAKECH
ROUTE AL BLYD, EN DIRECTION DE FÈS
10 km from Marrakesh

ramakech.com
Instagram:
@ramakech_parcdesscultures

Visits: from Wednesday to Sunday
Admission: from 270 dirhams
Sidecar tours available by reservation through marrakechinsiders.com (5,300 dirhams per 2-person sidecar)

23

MADE IN MARRAKESH

On the outskirts of the city, the industrial district of Sidi Ghanem is an artisanal enclave brimming with designer workshops, trendy boutiques and showrooms of all kinds. A bustling hive where you can get your fill of inspiration strolling from interior-design shops to concept stores.

> **Marrakshi Life**

Since 2013, New York designer Randal Bachner has been leading the way when it comes to responsible and sustainable fashion. Imported from Egypt and Turkey, the cotton he uses is woven and dyed directly in the workshops of his brand, Marrakshi Life. Here everything is transformed and nothing is thrown away. Come visit his studio and discover all the manufacturing processes involved, from the creation of the fabric to the final product.

MARRAKSHI LIFE
933 ROUTE DE SAFI,
AL MASSAR INDUSTRIAL DISTRICT

Dh Dh Dh

+212 7 71 61 36 02	Instagram: @marrakshi.life	marrakshilife.com

© LRNCE STUDIO

> **LRNCE Studio**

You'll find nothing but beautiful things at Belgian designer Laurence Leenaert's boutique: ceramics, pillows, kimonos and leather bags inspired by Moroccan folklore and spiced up with an extremely modern graphic touch.

LRNCE STUDIO
59 RUE SIDI GHANEM

Dh Dh

Instagram: @lrnce

lrnce.com

> Le Magasin Général

Standing and ceiling fans, Chesterfield sofas, travel trunks ... The list of treasures available at Le Magasin Général (General Store) is seemingly never-ending. A small tour of this 'curiosity cabinet', with its faintly colonial atmosphere, is a must.

LE MAGASIN GÉNÉRAL
281 ROUTE DE SAFI,
SIDI GHANEM

Dh Dh

+212 5 24 33 66 73

Instagram: @magasin_general_marrakech
magasin-general-marrakech.com

> Galerie Pop

In a large white loft, Galerie Pop brings together Moroccan and foreign designers, artisans, retailers and artists. Halfway between a showroom and an art gallery, this artsy cave is packed with accessories, ceramics and designer furniture.

GALERIE POP
109-4 AVENUE PRINCIPALE
SIDI GHANEM

Dh Dh Dh

+212 5 24 33 60 08

Instagram: @galerie_pop

AIR FRANCE
AFRIQUE DU NORD
EXPOSITION COLONIALE
MARSEILLE
1922
COURRIER SUD

> **Riad Yima**

It's all there: the colours, posing visitors and crème de la kitsch. Tucked away behind the Place des Épices (Square of the Spice Sellers), Riad Yima is a reflection of its creator: extravagant and multicultural. Renovated in 2006 by the artist Hassan Hajjaj, who needs no introduction, this traditional old house, which still calls itself a riad even though it no longer serves as a guest house, has become a sanctuary of Moroccan–Warholian pop art.

Almost everything here is for sale. You can wander around the house, from art gallery to tea room, browse in the shop or take a Berber cooking class with the in-house cordon bleu. A must-see, right in the city centre.

The Moroccan pop art pioneer has just opened a new space, **Jajjah**, that's as colourfully hybrid as his first one in the industrial district of Sidi Ghanem.

There's a tea room with his brand of drinks, Jajjah, a restaurant that pays tribute to the dishes of his childhood and, needless to say, an exhibition space where you can discover his latest creations.

GALLERY-TEA ROOM RIAD YIMA
52 DERB AARJANE RAHBA LAKDIMA
MEDINA

+212 5 24 39 19 87

Instagram: @riadyima
riad-yima.com
contact@riadyima.com

JAJJAH CAFÉ
114-116 RUE SIDI GHANEM

Dh Dh

+212 5 24 33 65 37
Instagram: @jajjah.tea

HASSAN HAJJAJ
HASSAN HAJJAJ KESH ANGELS
BY HASSAN HAJJAJ
HASSAN HAJJAJ KESH ANGELS

HASSAN HAJJAJ

> **Lalla**

In the Sidi Ghanem industrial zone, Lalla has set up its new headquarters (part boutique, part showroom, part design studio) as an extension of its original Guéliz address. Here you can discover its vibrant world of terry-cloth bags and pouches made in Marrakesh, often lined with African wax-print fabrics.

LALLA
SHOWROOM: 280 SIDI GHANEM
GUÉLIZ BOUTIQUE: 35, BOULEVARD EL MANSOUR EDDAHBI

Dh Dh

Instagram: @lallamarrakech | shoplalla.com

> Marie Bastide

Marie Bastide's boutique in the Guéliz neighbourhood is a luminous white space with graceful curves flowing across three storeys. The ground floor is filled with handcrafted pieces such as silk scarves, raffia baskets, stitched leather goods and carved wooden animals. Downstairs you'll find a display of photographs and prints; upstairs is the design studio. Everything created by this lovely brand is made locally, bringing a refined and sensitive aesthetic to traditional Moroccan artisanship.

MARIE BASTIDE
GUÉLIZ BOUTIQUE: 32 RUE DE LA LIBERTÉ
MEDINA BOUTIQUE: 34 RUE DERB JDID

Dh Dh

Instagram: @mariebastidemarrakech

mariebastidemarrakech.com

#24

AN OASIS OF CALM
15 MINUTES
FROM THE CENTRE

Just 15 minutes from the city centre, Beldi Country Club is a genuine oasis where you could happily lose track of time. You'll find rooms surrounded by greenery; a souk stocking rugs, pottery, embroidery and beautiful hand-blown glassware at very reasonable prices; magnificent gardens; several swimming pools, two of them heated in winter (and what a pleasure, even at that time of year, to go for an after-breakfast swim!); a spa; a padel court and state-of-the-art gym equipment, and more. Lunch by one of the gorgeous pools is a real treat too. An absolute winner!

BELDI COUNTRY CLUB MARRAKECH
KM 6 ROUTE DU BARRAGE, CHERIFIA

+212 5 24 38 39 50 | Instagram: @beldicountryclub | beldicountryclub.com
contact@beldicountryclub.com

© ERIC MARTIN

© KAMAL WADIFI

25

A GARDEN **AS A SURREALIST WORK OF ART**

Here's an unusual garden that will be a hit on your Instagram page! A maze of prickly plants interspersed with surrealist sculptures, this botanical scene is the brainchild of the Austrian artist André Heller. Just 30 minutes from Marrakesh, this African Garden of Eden is a true green gem, the ideal destination for an afternoon of fresh air.

After wandering around, stop for a snack at the Paul Bowles café while admiring the view of the Atlas Mountains.

ANIMA
DOUAR SBITI, ROUTE D'OURIKA

+212 6 66 56 17 76	Instagram: @animagardenofficial info@anima-garden.com anima-garden.com	Admission from 6€ (free shuttle from Marrakesh included in the price of the ticket)

© SUZY STÖCKL

#26

ROOMS YOU'LL REMEMBER FOR THE REST OF YOUR LIFE

From romantic villas to ultra-local B&Bs, from Andalusian palaces to traditional riads, Marrakesh is teeming with an exceptional range of accommodation – you'll find some of the most incredible options outside the city.

> The favourite retreat of aesthetes

This retreat is set in the foothills of the mountains, in the idyllic Ourika Valley. Only 35 minutes from Marrakesh, these eco-friendly Berber lodges offer a radical change of scenery for anyone wanting to escape from the urban chaos for a bit.

KASBAH BAB OURIKA
VALLÉE OURIKA, TNINE OURIKA
40 kilometers from Marrakesh

+212 6 68 74 95 47

bookings@kasbahbabourika.com
kasbahbabourika.com
Instagram: @kasbahbabourika

From 150€ (double) to 1,650€ (private villa with swimming pool) per night
Three-night minimum stay

© LA PAUSE

> **The new nomadism**

Deep in the dunes of the Agafay Desert, La Pause lives up to its name. While there's no electricity or air conditioning here, what you will find is the absolute charm of a candlelit dinner and a night spent in a tent, like the nomads of old.

LA PAUSE
DOUAR LMIH LAROUSSIENE, AGAFAY DESERT
35 kilometers from Marrakesh

Reservation on +212 6 10 77 22 40	Instagram: @lapausemarrakech	lapause1@gmail.com lapause-marrakech.com

> The rural retreat

From its hilltop, Kasbah Beldi offers an astounding view of the desert and Lalla Takerkoust Lake. Located just 50 minutes from Marrakesh, this old farm provides a breath of fresh air for anyone wishing to escape the city to spend a night under the Moroccan stars.

KASBAH BELDI
LALLA TAKERKOUST LAKE, TALET
65 kilometers from Marrakesh

+212 5 24 38 39 50	Instagram: @kasbahbeldi	contact@kasbahbeldi.com kasbahbeldi.com

> **Glamping in the dunes**

Lost in the lunar landscape of the Agafay Desert, the unbleached tents of Scarabeo Camp stand out against the majestic Atlas Mountains. Sitting by a campfire, you'll feel almost like you're one of the region's first explorers.

© SCARABEO CAMP

SCARABEO CAMP
AGAFAY DESERT
35 kilometers from Marrakesh

+212 8 08 50 53 15

Instagram: @scarabeo_camp

scarabeocamp.com
info@scarabeo-camp.com

> **A boutique hotel in the desert**

Driving along the small *route provinciale*, after 30 minutes, small houses made of terracotta and tadelakt come into view. This is the refuge of the Franco-Swiss architect Romain Michel-Ménière. A place of simple elegance, where the only obvious luxury is a swimming pool, ideal for cooling off on days when the scorching *sharqī* wind sweeps across the Atlas plains.

BERBER LODGE
DOUAR OUMNES, TAMESLOTH
30 kilometers from Marrakesh

+212 6 62 04 90 43 | Instagram: @berberlodge_ | hotelberberlodge@gmail.com berberlodge.net

Here's a playlist to accompany you on your peregrinations around this magical city. It's a mix of Gnawa songs, minimal Eastern reveries, and traditional and contemporary sounds ... To us, it represents the aural complexity of Morocco, somewhere between musicological deep dive and electronic modernity: https://tinyurl.com/a66wt4fv

THE SOUNDS OF MARRAKESH

Discovering Moroccan music is reason enough to travel there. Nourished by centuries of history, Islamisation, cultural exchange and intense artistic creation, the country's musical heritage is infinitely rich. Whether it's boisterous rhythms or languid rhapsodies, there's a sound to accompany every great moment in life, as well as all the little everyday things. The following is a short, non-exhaustive guide to immersing yourself in this musical odyssey.

> Once the chant of Berber shepherds, *raï* was propelled into the international arena in the 1990s by figures like Cheb Mami. Rebellious and modern, this music belongs to Morocco's youth.

> While there are many (more or less traditional) styles of *chaabi* in Morocco; it's often played at weddings and is always popular party music. The lyrics are light-hearted and the steps set to the rhythm of a *darbuka*, the goblet drum favoured by *chaabi* musicians.

> *Dakka marrakchia* is the characteristic ritual and folk music of Marrakesh, somewhere between religious incantation and African trance. Frenetic and mystical in equal measure.

> An integral part of Muslim spirituality, Sufi music is sacred. Sufi brotherhoods sometimes give concerts; otherwise, head to the Samaa Festival of Sacred Music in autumn.

> *Malhun* is sung poetry that touches on virtually every aspect and concern in the everyday life of Moroccans. A spontaneous, poetic and intergenerational art form, it has adapted perfectly to modern times. A kind of popular poetry slam.

> Widely popularised by the Gnaoua World Music Festival, which has been held in Essaouira every year since 1998, Gnaoua music has been classified as Intangible Cultural Heritage by UNESCO. On Jemaa el Fnaa square, you'll find Gnaoua musicians moving to the sound of their *guembri* (or *sintir*), the instrument they use in all their rites.

In this collection, the last address won't always be revealed because it's too confidential. Up to you to find it!

#27

MOHAMED BARIZ, THE VOICE OF MOROCCO

Once upon a time, there was Mohamed Bariz, who tells his country's most beautiful stories. When he was just 12 years old, he was already captivating passers-by on Jemaa el Fnaa square, keeping alive an art that barely survives in Morocco today. Forty years later, he still performs in Arabic, French and English at festivals around the world as one of the last representatives of this ancient tradition of itinerant storytelling. He's fighting body and soul to save this fragile art, and the best way you can support him in this struggle is by listening to him and allowing him to remind you of your childhood dreams.

To meet this unique soul, ask around at the stalls on Jemaa el Fnaa square; the orange-juice sellers might let you know where you can find him ...

Tales in Arabic, French and English

ACKNOWLEDGEMENTS

Fabrice would like to thank:

ZOHAR for having shared *his* Marrakesh with me and for the beautiful moments of laughter and friendship experienced there.

LUCIE for her invaluable help with the texts, her unflagging good mood and for dealing with my eternal geographic and scheduling confusion.

OKSANA for having spent many hours gathering a great deal of valuable practical information.

ALL OUR MARRAKSHI FRIENDS for their generosity, openness, willingness to share and ability to reveal this city in all its richness and complexity.

Zohar would like to thank:

FABRICE for bringing me into this project and allowing me to rediscover a city that's so close to my heart and soul.

ABDELAALI AIT KARROUM, our photographer, for his patience and for continually finding creative ways to shoot a city in the midst of a pandemic.

ANNAELLE MYRIAM CHAAIB (aka Myriam au citron), our talented illustrator, for her courage and for bringing colour and warmth to this book with her 'naïf'-style depictions of Marrakesh.

MY MOTHER, THE SLAOUI FAMILY, AMINE KABBAJ AND AMINE BENDRIOUICH for holding my hand through the proverbial secret alleyways of Marrakesh and astonishing me each time with new discoveries that delight the eye and new encounters that renew your faith in the magic of travel.

Thomas Jonglez would like to thank:

JULIE and **ALEXANDRE LEYMARIE**, as well as **AURORE CHAFFANGEON**, for her contribution to 'Les Étoiles de Jemaa el-Fna' and her valuable advice.

This book was created by:
Fabrice Nadjari, Zohar Benjelloun and Aurore Chaffangeon, authors
Abdelaali Ait Karroum, photos (unless otherwise stated)
Annaelle Myriam Chaaib, illustrations
Emmanuelle Willard Toulemonde, layout
Sophie Schlondorff and Olivia Fuller, translation
Jana Gough, copy-editing
Dikshit Akbari, proofreading
Mado de La Quintinie, publishing

Cover photo: © Adobe Stock / Hortigüela

You can write to us at info@jonglezpublishing.com
Follow us on Instagram: @jonglez_publishing

THANK YOU

From the same publisher

Photo Books

Abandoned America: The age of Consequences
Abandoned Asylums
Abandoned Australia
Abandoned Belgium
Abandoned Churches: Unclaimed Places of Worship
Abandoned Cinemas of the World
Abandoned France
Abandoned Germany
Abandoned Lebanon
Abandoned Italy
Abandoned Japan
Abandoned Spain
Abandoned USSR
Abandoned World – An AI-generated exploration
After the Final Curtain: The Fall of the American Movie Theater
After the Final Curtain: America's Abandoned Theaters
Baikonur – Vestiges of the Soviet Space Program
Cinemas – A French Heritage
Chernobyl's Atomic Legacy – 25 years after disaster
Clickbait – A visual journey through AI-generated stories
Destination: Wellness – Our 35 best places in the world to take time out
Forbidden Places – Exploring our Abandoned Heritage
Forgotten Heritage
Oblivion
Parisian Theatres – Exceptional Venues
Secret Art Nouveau
Secret Sacred Sites
The cinemas of India – An exceptional heritage
Venice deserted
Venice from the skies

'Confidential' and 'Soul of' Guides

Berlin Confidential
Lisbon Confidential
Los Angeles Confidential
Malta Confidential
Munich Confidential
New York City Confidential
Paris Confidential

Soul of Amsterdam - A guide to the 30 best experiences
Soul of Athens – 30 experiences
Soul of Barcelona – 30 experiences
Soul of Brussels – A guide to exceptional experiences
Soul of Detroit – A guide to exceptional experiences
Soul of Kyoto – A guide to exceptional experiences
Soul of Marseille – A guide to exceptional experiences
Soul of Milan – A guide to exceptional experiences
Soul of Rome – A guide to exceptional experiences
Soul of Tokyo – A guide to exceptional experiences
Soul of Venice – A guide to exceptional experiences
Soul of Vienna – A guide to exceptional experiences

Atlases of curiosities

Atlas of extreme weather
Atlas of forbidden places
Atlas of geographical curiosities
Atlas of geographical curiosities – Britain
Atlas of unusual wines
Atlas of urban vineyards

Secret atlases

Berlin – The secret atlas
London – The secret atlas
New York – The secret atlas
Paris – The secret atlas
Rome – The secret atlas
Venice – The secret atlas

'Secret' Guides

Secret Amsterdam
Secret Bali – An unusual guide
Secret Bangkok
Secret Barcelona
Secret Bars & Restaurants in Paris
Secret Bath – An unusual guide
Secret Belfast
Secret Berlin
Secret Boston – An unusual guide
Secret Brighton – An unusual guide
Secret Brooklyn
Secret Brussels
Secret Budapest
Secret Buenos Aires
Secret Campania
Secret Cape Town
Secret Copenhagen
Secret Corsica
Secret Dolomites
Secret Dublin – An unusual guide
Secret Edinburgh – An unusual guide
Secret Florence
Secret French Riviera
Secret Geneva
Secret Glasgow – An unusual guide
Secret Granada
Secret Helsinki
Secret Istanbul
Secret Johannesburg
Secret Kuala Lumpur
Secret Lisbon
Secret Liverpool – An unusual guide
Secret London – An unusual guide
Secret London – Unusual Bars & Restaurants
Secret Los Angeles – An unusual guide
Secret Louisiana
Secret Madrid
Secret Mexico City
Secret Milan
Secret Montreal – An unusual guide
Secret Naples
Secret New Orleans – An unusual guide
Secret New York – An unusual guide
Secret New York – Curious Activities
Secret New York – Hidden Bars & Restaurants
Secret Normandy
Secret Paris
Secret Potsdam
Secret Prague
Secret Provence
Secret Rio
Secret Rome
Secret Seville
Secret Singapore
Secret Stockholm
Secret Strasbourg
Secret Sussex – An unusual guide
Secret Tokyo
Secret Tuscany
Secret Venice
Secret Venice Lagoon
Secret Vienna
Secret Washington DC – An unusual guide
Secret York – An unusual guide

Registration of copyright: September 2026 – Edition: 01
ISBN: 978-2-38715-078-3
Printed in June 2026 in Bulgaria by Dedrax